THE BARB IN THE RHYME

POEMS

BY

JEAN HILL

Other work by Jean Hill

"The Sting In The Tale"

**Poems and Short Stories
To make you laugh and cry**

**Available from: Lulu.com
or
Amazon**

IN THE BEGINNING

Things have moved on since the publication of my first book "The Sting In The Tale". As a regular guest speaker at social events, I am invariably asked "When did you start writing poetry?"

Well, I have written poetry since childhood. My first poem, written in beautiful copperplate, was called "Embarrassing for Nanny". It was inspired by my lovely Victorian grand-mother, a somewhat over-weight lady, struggling up the steps of a trolley-bus with a broken suspender. For those who don't remember, stockings used to be held up by suspenders. The poem got me into a lot of trouble and was not as well received as my nine-year-old heart desired! My mother thought it was very rude and my grand-mother threatened me with "Big Tom" which was a cane she kept hanging up behind the cupboard door but thankfully never used!

In those days to speak of any part of one's physical anatomy was taboo. To use ugly words like "tits" or "bum" would have labelled you a "gutter-snipe" and earned you a clip around the ear. Worse words were unheard of!

The "mat" in my poem refers to a length of hessian my grand-mother had bought; no doubt for my mother to make into a rag-rug to put in front of the fire. My only change to the poem is to include an apostrophe to indicate the missing first syllable of the word "suspender". As a child I thought the word was "spender". Otherwise it is unchanged.

What's the saying "From little acorns, etc......?" Well, on that scale I'm probably about twig size now, so if you've still the will, thank you for turning the page and reading my first infamous poem.

This photo is of my younger sister, Lynda, and me on holiday in Hastings in 1952.
We spent all our holidays sitting in a shelter on the sea-front.

Embarrassing for Nanny

Nanny's 'spender came undone
And in a shelter she had fun
When at last she'd done it up
The other one did come unstuck

Nothing happened for a while at all
Then her knickers began to fall
Was her face so very red
As out of them she tried to tread

Off she walked along the prom'
Poor Nanny had no knickers on
And when a gust of wind did blow
She tried to cover what did show

That great strong wind, it blew and blew
Until she didn't know what to do
And when at last she caught the bus
A crowd of people were following us

Nanny sat right at the back
And up her skirt she stuffed a mat
Nan gave the conductor quite a fright
As under the seat she crouched from sight

The scandal in the local papers
Gave a detailed description of Nanny's capers
Always remember, if you can
Take a pin, be prepared, not like Nan

By Jean Constance Marchant
(Aged 9)

ACKNOWLEDGEMENTS

Deborah and **Samantha** ... for being so hugely supportive in the practical production of this second book. Without your skill and patience it would never have happened.

Sharon ... for continued encouragement.

Robin ... for the front cover photography.

Benjamin and **Jamie** ... for just being.

THANK – YOU ALL

A CORGI CALLED MONTY

There's a vacancy at the palace
Live in with all meals free
"Must like dogs" the advert said
So I sent them my C.V.

Now I'm appointed under-footman
And in palace hierarchy
That's one step up from frog-spawn
In the below-stairs malarkey

I'm a personal attendant
In my velvet flunkeys suit
To her Maj's favourite corgi
A vicious little brute

At six o'clock each morning
Round the garden we must go
But he doesn't want to get up
So I help him with my toe

It's a quick run round the flower-beds
Then I shut him in the shed
With doggy-chocs and Winalot
Then creep back to my warm bed

Monty's fed on finest food-stuff
(It's just beans on toast for me)
So I swipe his beef and rabbit
And I eat it for my tea

I exercise him daily
And when he's scoffed his grub
I tie him to my mud-guard
And then cycle to the pub

Each day at four precisely
All brushed, bright-eyed and clean
I present this pampered corgi
To Her Majesty, the Queen

She said "Sit beside me Monty dear"
I warned her not to risk it
'Cos the greedy little blighter
Snapped her garibaldi biscuit

She jumped up with alacrity
Well, at her age they don't come fitter
And although I begged her pardon, M'am
It wasn't me that bit her

With royal digit blue-blood dripping
If she'd had it in her power
I'd be hung, drawn and quartered
And shackled in the tower

Her Maj said it was all my fault
Now my position is diminished
And my days as under-footman
Have been and gone and finished

Monty? - He received a pardon
The mutt could do no wrong
Her Maj gave him a cuddle
And a silver doggy gong

So now when they troop the colour
I walk behind a mounted trooper
With a dirty great big shovel
And a horse-size pooper-scooper

AUNTIE MILDRED'S BOX

Poor Auntie Mildred died last week
And to heaven she was sent
Now the relatives have gathered
To hear her will and testament

With haste she was cremated
And her ashes duly scattered
And with greedy eyes of avarice
What she's left is all that mattered

The family sat around the table
All sure that they'd inherit
They'd sent her the odd Christmas card
To stand them in good merit

The solicitor sat before them
What's the matter with the bloke?
Surely his eyes hold amusement
But with solemnity he spoke

He opened up the parchment
A new will signed last week
An expectant hush descended
As he proceeded then to speak

"We are gathered here together
And now the time has come
To read the will of Mildred
Who died aged ninety-one"

They said "Shame she's kicked the bucket
Of course we're all bereft
But get a move on Matey
And tell us what she's left"

So in the words of Mildred
Of sound mind and very clear
She told them all to sod-off
'Cos she didn't want them here

She said "I've left you nothing
I've spent it all on gin"
Well, with outrage all-consuming
You'd hear the dropping of a pin

There was only one true mourner
And although not orthodox
Sat her scruffy mongrel, Fido
Guarding Mildred's secret box

But the solicitor hadn't finished
There was more that must be said
"Someone go get Mildred's box
Hidden there in the dog's bed

We need someone with courage
Who'll run the risk of teeth filled jaws
And retrieve the little wooden box
From between old Fido's paws"

And so the box was bravely snatched
Then placed before the man of law
And he produced a tiny silver key
To open up a secret drawer

Relatives watched with bated breath
For him to turn the key and click it
And there safely tucked within the box
Was a winning lottery ticket

The solicitor surveyed them
If they thought they'd get a share
Their greedy scheming wishes
Would vanish in thin air

Aunt Mildred's voice resounded
Said "In my old-age years
I had just one loyal and faithful friend
To share love and joy and tears

With unconditional devotion
No more loneliness would enter
Our final sad and empty years
With Fido - from the rescue centre

So with this winning ticket
I'm buying a dogs' home
And dear Fido, live in luxury
And buy each dog there a bone

And to those gathered round this table
There's only one more thing to say
In life learn well this lesson
Every dog must have its day"

Auntie Mildred smiled on high
(She got on well with God)
She left her folk a flea in their ear
And everything else to the dog

The family all spat feathers
Saying "Take the box and bin it"
But Fido hung on grimly
It had Mildred's smell within it

Everyone left, the wooden box closed
The secret now was told
Her best friend gobbled rump steak
Off a plate of solid gold

And Fido spent his twilight years
In comfort: I'm delighted
Now dog and box with Mildred
Are in heaven - reunited

BASSETT'S BABY

My husband looked at our new baby
His face a puzzled frown
Asked: "Why, with my complexion ivory
Is the baby blackish brown?"

He said: "Your eyes are pale sky blue
And we're both blond and fair
How is it our new baby
Has frizzy jet black hair?"

Silly boy – I smiled so sweetly
Waved away his worried thoughts
The explanation's clearly obvious
It's all those liquorice allsorts!

<u>CHANGING FORCE</u>

The avuncular policeman image
Now exists in times long gone
When a simple clip around the ear
Would sort out right from wrong

Times have changed – it's sad to say
Now we face terrorist attacks
But we expect the police to be there
Keep us safe; to watch our backs

They might have high-tech uniforms
But no matter what they wear
It won't protect from knife or bullet
As they go where we don't dare

Some police may carry Tasers
Or canisters of gas
But is that enough deterrent
When faced with mobs en-masse?

While we applaud their bravery
The sad fact is the day may come
When all our British Police Force
Need be issued with a gun

CHRISTMAS ROUND ROBIN

Do you get those Christmas missives
From folk you hardly know
That relate their year in detail
Step-by-step and blow-by-blow

Thank you for your Christmas message
I'm relieved that you are free
From the trials and tribulations
That affect the likes of me

I'm glad to hear your family
Has talent oozing out its pores
With your wet-room and your au-pair
And your Georgian style front doors

To know your husband's made a million
In the banking world is mega
It brings a gladness to my heart
'Cos mine's a lazy beggar

My old man don't fancy working
The dole money don't go far
Nice you've got a new Mercedes
We had the wheels nicked off our car

So you've cruised the Caribbean
And you've skied off-piste in Jackson
Us - we had a wet and windy week
In a boarding house in Clacton

To learn that your son Tristram
Has nine straight A's in Latin
And Lucinda expelled triplets
In the birthing pool she sat in

Our Kylie's had a baby too
Funny looking – but a big 'un
Its Dad's a traffic warden
Some bloke she met in Wigan

I'm thrilled your cousin's grandad
So bravely looped-the-loop
In a glider made of balsa wood
Without a parachute

It's nice your sister Zara
Flies the world in a jet plane
Our Mavis is a hostess too
With punters – on the game

Our Wayne's well into gardening
He's ordered lots of seed
Now we've a hot-house in the yard
He's growing his own weed

Grandad's no longer with us
A heart-attack – dropped dead
When the stripper sat upon his lap
In our local – The Nag's Head

Our Norman's doing pretty well
From petty crime he's risen
With his extended education
In the young offenders' prison

As for me - I'm not complaining
But life's become no joke
And if I don't win at Bingo
I'm always stony broke

But I can't remember who you are
I just can't place your name
I don't think our paths will ever cross
But Merry Christmas just the same

(All characters are of the writer's bizarre imagination)

D.I.Y. MURDER

I'm going to murder my husband
One day he's going to cop it
In a frenzy of frustration
I'll grab his head and whop it

He's taken up with D.I.Y.
Thinks he's an expert who
Can fix things that need fixing
With nails and screws and glue

He's bought himself a manual
And now that winter's coming
He's busy lagging all the pipes
And sorting out the plumbing

So in a cold spell after Christmas
When all the pipes did freeze
You'd think that he'd know what to do
With all that expertise

Well, he ripped up all the carpet
The floor-boards came up next
I wasn't very happy
In fact I was quite vexed

With the frozen pipe located
And blasted with hot air
We soon had water running
I'll say that – to be fair

Then he put the floor-boards back
And secured them good and tight
But hammered in the final nail
Right through the water pipe

He poked his finger in the hole
It stopped the flow all right
But I couldn't get a plumber
So I left him there all night

The manual didn't help much
He re-read on how to plumb
And finally he plugged the hole
With a lump of chewing gum

We put new carpet in the bedroom
It had a slightly thicker weave
But the door then wouldn't open
Even though I'd shove and heave

So he took it off its hinges
Cut off the bottom – quite a lot
But still it didn't open
The dope cut it off the top

Then with rawl plugs at the ready
I said "Hang the clock up there"
He drilled through a mains cable
Catapulted off the chair

With electric sparks and flashes
And static in his hair
He never quite made heaven
But he hurtled through the air

The house was plunged in darkness
And I know without a doubt
'Cos neighbours were complaining
That he put the street-lamps out

Now he's buying plugs and sockets
The electrics to re-wire
To modernize the circuits
And the artificial fire

He's bought paint and poly-filler
Says he'll decorate and plaster
And our house is like a war zone
It's a D.I.Y. disaster

Today he's cleaning gutters
And the drain-pipe on the wall
He poked it with a big stick
And out shot a tennis ball

Then he peered up the down-pipe
And before a word was said
Half a ton of slimy gunge
Whooshed out on his head

He stood inside the kitchen
And dripped on my clean tiles
And divested all his clothing
Into smelly little piles

And now he's gone to have a wash
The water's on full power
But when he comes down I'll kill him
'Cos he's blocking up the shower

I've had enough – my nerves have twanged
The answer's homicide
I planned his extermination
The last time he D.I.Y'ed

I'll get his head in his own vice
And then I'm going to whack it
I'll stuff him in a suitcase
And hide him in the attic

Or I could feed him rhubarb leaves
And when he starts to stagger
I'd garrotte him with his plumb line
Or push him off his ladder

And if I'm ever brought to justice
With my worn and haggard look
With luck I'll get a female judge
Who'll let me off the hook

She'll see me as a victim
A "Do-It-Yourself" rebel
And with suffering wives behind her
She'll award me with a medal

(Any resemblance to a real person is purely intentional)

DAFFODILS

Yes, I'm in there with Wordsworth
His host of golden daffodils
Heralding the Spring-time
A sight that always thrills

So when I find eternal rest
And released from worldly ills
Please place upon my headstone
One hundred daffodils.

DON'T TAKE ME HIKING

My little feet so soft and clean
Daily smoothed with Nivea cream
Gently massaged in the sink
Pearly toenails painted pink
With pumice stone there's no hard skin
In a beauty contest my feet would win
No sign of bunions or cracked heels
No verruca, corns, and that reveals
The cushioned sheltered life they've led
From get up time 'til they're in bed
I thought they'd always stay that way
'Til we took a hiking holiday

In thick green socks and clumpy boots
I've trudged up hills and tripped on roots
Ploughed through mud and muck and mire
I've put my feet through conditions dire
I've slid through smelly slurry-slime
Now between my toes there nestles grime
My pinkie toenails rimmed with black
Have I walked bare-foot on nutty-slack
I've blisters on my heels for sure
And my poor feet are red and raw
Clod-hopping boots round ankles laced
With nine more bloody miles I'm faced

I thought this holiday would be
A voyage of discovery
I've discovered hiking's what I hate
And if you still want to be my mate
Book me into a hotel that's clean
And bring a chiropodist on the scene
Bring me a foot-spa and perfumed soap
And send for a taxi now – you dope
Take off my boots – they're soddened through
Remove my mud-caked trousers too
Then take a hike – and don't come back
Or I'll strangle you with your rucksack strap

FAILING FACULTIES

My faculties are failing
I've arthritis in my knees
And now I get these dizzy spells
My chest tightens and I wheeze

I've got osteoporosis
But at my age I shouldn't grumble
But if I try to turn my head
My neck bones start to crumble

With cramp my legs lock solid
It's the statin pills I blame
As I stagger on the pavement
With my trusty Zimmer frame

Both my ears have packed up
I can't hear a word you say
I take twenty-seven different pills
To get me through each day

And now I've got these cataracts
And I can't see very far
But at least I've got my licence
So I can drive the car

<u>FAIR COP</u>

There's a speed cop right behind me
And he's sitting on my tail
I can see his blue light flashing
I can hear his siren wail

I'm doing forty in a thirty
I'm on a sticky wicket
He's pulled along beside me
And I've got a speeding ticket

The system shows no mercy
I've got to pay the fine
Instead of doing thirty now
I'll stick to twenty-nine

FAIR SHARES

My husband got this common itch
We'd been married seven years
He's run off with a Barbie Doll
And left me here in tears

She's young and blonde ... and tarty
And she flaunts a "wiggle" bum
I feel old and fat and forty
With stretch marks on my tum

He's got this Porsche – his pride and joy
With body gleaming red
He's left it in the garage
With a note – here's what he said

"We'll divvy-up the assets
You can sell that Porsche of mine
Get as much as you can for it
And transfer the cash on-line"

So I sold it for a fiver
To a dealer mean and shifty
And when I deducted my share
I sent him two pounds fifty.

FIGHTING FIT

Me and my friend Ethel
We're both keep fit fanatics
With aerobics and fast walking
And a spot of acrobatics

One night out exercising
Two yobs followed in our wake
Their intention was to mug us
A really big mistake

So I shook my head at Ethel
Said: It's our duty to correct 'em
We swung our size eight walking boots
And their teeth shot out their rectum

FINANCIAL PLANNING

I've saved up for my retirement
Put by a sum quite tidy
I've enough to live in luxury
If I plan to die by Friday

FOR THE LOVE OF MY VIXEN

Are you sitting comfortably?
Little fox-cubs gather round
And let your father tell you
Of his escape from horse and hound

In the mist the brass horn sounding
As I fearfully left my earth
To lead the hunt to pastures far
While my vixen mate gave birth

With all my senses buzzing
I could hear their hue and cry
That day I'd father new-born cubs
Or would it be the day I'd die

I counted my pursuers
There mounted – ten of them
Three ruthless horsey women
And seven savage red-clad men

First I headed for the cliff top
And at the edge I swiftly swerved
I'm glad to say the horse stopped
But Colonel Blimp flew like a bird

Led by Lady Daphne Floggit
The unspeakably evil nine
Chased me off towards the shore-line
Through the high and foaming brine

I knew for sure that horses swim
But Daphne Floggit, although brave
Catapulted o'er her horse's head
And drowned in a six foot wave

Next I headed for the forest
You should have heard the vicar holler
Got caught up in the branches
Garrotted by his own dog collar

The hypocrites on Sunday
Sing "All Creatures Great and Small"
Then pursue their gruesome blood-lust
While the good Lord loves us all

But then the hunt continued
And I'm chased through marshes dire
Sir Twiglet's horse – it bolted
Flung him head-first in the mire

The odds were still uneven
With six remaining in the saddle
So I raced across the quick-sand
And I took them for a paddle

The plan worked well – the heaviest lump
The Honourable Plankton-Smythe
Got stuck up to his arm-pits
And faced a fast in-coming tide

Joining in the hunt that day
Was Wayne Bloggs, a lottery winner
He came hoping for an invite
To the manor for his dinner

So I led him through the meadow
Where a great big black bull dwells
Shame I couldn't wait around
To hear his screams and yells

But my energy was flagging
There were still four in the chase
More wily skills need be employed
I meant to win that race

So I headed for the hedgerows
Where the undergrowth was dense
But sadly that remaining few
Had more blood-lust than sense

Dame Felicity Prudence Flunket
Featured in The Hound and Whippet
Impaled her vast proportions
On a vicious thorny thicket

I dived across some train lines
Whoosh! – so close, my senses reeling
And poor old Major Cough-Drop
Caught the one-fifteen to Ealing

I had to keep on running
Couldn't stop – no time to wait
There's still a high-class trollop saddled
And a pompous magistrate

So I dashed across the golf course
On to where they're playing cricket
The bimbo did a "maiden over"
And hit upon a sticky wicket

And the final young blood out there
Well, he thought he was a winner
But the hounds had all been cheated
So they ate him for their dinner

Exhausted I trudged homeward
But delight – waiting there for me
Was my vixen, yes – your mother
And to my joy – you three

In this world there is much suffering
That men still perpetrate
Where there could be love and laughter
They nurture cruelty and hate

And so we live another day
But as I'm labelled such a sinner
I'll nip behind the farmer's shed
And grab a chicken for our dinner

(Through the Eyes of Wilfred the Fox)

FULL CIRCLE

When I was a youngster
There was a rule to be observed
That all the little children
Should be seen but never heard

Now it's come round full circle
I've lived some ninety years
As I lie here in my 'care' bed
And I'm seen but no-one hears

HAIKU THOUGHTS

Look into man's soul
Is his tread heavy or light
Burdened or carefree

Judge not or be judged
Be not the first to throw stones
Platitudes placate

We turn a blind eye
Should we turn the other cheek
Let conscience decide

Why not throw the stone
Someone must blow the whistle
Put up or shut-up

Speak out and protect
Society's meek and frail
Do not still your voice

Seeking amnesty
In a populace of sheep
Heralds destruction

Let stillness invade
Action will be salvation
And peace your reward

HIGH HOPES

I'm grateful to the government
For giving back to me
The right to keep on working
At the age of eighty-three

So I dug out the sequinned leotard
And before the mirror gave a twirl
Although the costume sagged a bit
Thought "You've still got it, girl"

They want a new pole dancer
In the night-club up the road
And now they've banned ageism
I can prove I'm not too old

So I went for my audition
And to the strains of King Creole
With a puff of my inhaler
I shimmied up the pole

I gyrated to the very top
But with a neat back-flip
I hurtled down the bloody pole
With a dislocated hip

Now I just have my pension
And the government's to blame
The only pole I dance round is
My trusty zimmer-frame

HIT BACK

I was the victim of a mugging
By a vicious little thug
With a tattoo and a hoodie
And an evil ugly mug

I'm not into forgiveness
Eye for eye is what I say
If I could get my hands on him
He'd live to rue the day

But he was duly apprehended
And off to jail he went
Now I've received this letter
From the prison he was sent

Asked do I want to meet him
No – I don't think it's befitting
Not unless a big and burly bloke
Could hold him while I hit 'im

Asked if I'd like to visit
And forgive him – No – Not me!
You can keep him in that prison
And throw away the key

HOMELESS

When we see a homeless person
On a blanket in the street
We might toss him some pennies
But our eyes – they never meet

We barely give a passing glance
And our thoughts we never hone
On what made this poor lad homeless
On the pavement all alone

Did his mother never want him
Or was he abused in care
Perhaps with mental issues
He has no future – just despair

Will he become a hardened vagrant
That society will shun
A life beneath the viaduct
Where rats and vermin run

Will he become a sad meths drinker
Reduced to skin and bone
While we can't look him in the eyes
He's beyond our comfort zone

<u>HORSE SENSE</u>

Please spare a thought for me – the horse
When I'm ridden round the roads
With headlights flashing up me back-side
Exhaust fumes fuming up me nose

I'd rather gallop fields of green
But I've got this stupid prat
Who steers me through the motor-cars
In jodhpurs and hard hat

Yes, I know I hold up traffic
Chill, relax, or sing a sonnet
Or I'll kick in your front bumper
And deposit on your bonnet

Remember that it's not my fault
It's this plonker in my saddle
Who waves and nods at motorists
As white lines they're forced to straddle

So please just keep your distance
When round the lanes I'm ploddin'
Don't rev and hoot your hooter
At me – old faithful Dobbin

IDENTITY CRISIS

With righteous indignation
And vitriolic prose
Filled with latent anger
'Cos it gets right up my nose
So here I'm going to let off steam
Before my gasket blows
And vent my suppressed feelings
So that everybody knows

When I was just a baby
My family christened me
Which embraced me as a member of
Christian Community
The vicar duly named me
And everyone could see
That I was welcomed to this land
Of Christianity

Now faced with officialdom
And required to fill a form
They ask me for my 'first' name
Well, that's become the norm
For Heaven's sake, I'm Christian
And when will that light dawn
To strike out 'first', write Christian
Is the vow that I've now sworn

'First', 'family', 'given', 'chosen'
Is surely not the same
When what the form should ask me is
'What is your *Christian* name?'
It's my heritage, my right
That I want to re-claim
When we lose our own traditions
We'll have just ourselves to blame

And when it comes to ethnicity
I don't even stop to think
Strike out 'white', 'black', or 'Asian'
Write English and Pale Pink
English values are important
Our country's on the brink
Of losing its own culture
And driving me to drink

I respect the right of others
To worship as they please
And I admit that I'm not 'churchy'
Rarely get down on my knees
And though my views are just my own
Not everyone agrees
England is a Christian country
With Christian identities

INFRA DIG

If you want to jet around the world
Fancy-free – without a care
You can choose your aviator
But your best bet is Brian-Air

We offer you the lowest prices
From two pounds, ninety-nine
Book a seat; it's very cheap
You can do it all on-line

There are some hidden extras
Like, should you need to use the loo
Or perhaps require a sick-bag
We charge fifty-pence for two.

There's a small charge for a seat belt
And the life jacket's no cheaper
But if you buy a package deal
We throw in whistle, light and bleeper

If you want to bring a suitcase
Or you'd like mushy peas to eat
You'll need to take a mortgage out
To afford that little treat

You could always book with Fly-Wee
They're a very small air-line
And with glue and strong elastic
We're sure you'll be just fine

If you choose Vermin Atlantic
Led by Rich with fungus face
You'll get media devices
Or a trip to outer-space

You can fly with Skittish Airways
They specialise long haul
Kuala Lumpur to Malawi
Timbuctoo to Montreal

They've stylish trolley dollies
But we want none of that
We've "thunder thighs" hostesses
Who fill the aisle with fatty slack

And our rival competition
Out there is Wheezy Jet
You're in safe hands with Stelios
Parachute and safety net

If you'd like to pay in drachma
Help the Greek economy
They'll serve taramasalata
And a dish of olives – free

But you're best off with Brian-Air
We've pilots fresh from college
They read their instruction manuals
To supplement their knowledge

The cuisine is unrivalled
Greasy burgers, pizza, baps
Coffee served in polystyrene
All dumped upon your laps

Our hostesses are all buxom
Shell-suit, trainers, peroxide hair
And with flashing, smiling dentures
Thank you for flying with Brian-Air

JAKEY AND JAS

I'm Jake, a powerful Labrador
As gentle as I'm strong
And with eyes like melting chocolate
I'm forgiven every wrong

My doggy-cousin, Jasmine
(Mischief is her middle-name)
She's a saucy little Yorkie
Always ready for a game

Jasmine having a "duvet-day"

I look after my Dad's chickens
But when Jasmine came to stay
She chased them round the garden
And for a week they didn't lay

We're chipped and vaccinated
A vet on hand to cure all ills
Our Mums and Dads work hard to pay
Our doggy-doctor bills

We're fed a healthy diet
Our weight is watched with care
And we keep our family near us
On the country walks we share

We're off to Gran and Grandad's
For a doggy holiday
We know they love to have us
As we brighten up their day

We bring fun to their retirement
Well, they've nothing else to do
They've time to wipe our muddy paws
And scoop up our doggy poo

Grandad's sorting out the Hoover
It's clogged up with doggy hairs
And when it comes to bed-time
We're the first ones up the stairs

I charge around their fish-pond
Through the roses Jasmine flies
We play ball with dear old Grandad
Just to keep him exercised

We let Grandad join in all our games
Especially hide and seek
We hid his slippers in the greenhouse
And he searched for them all week

I'm a friendly big black giant
But my bark's enough to scare
We keep the garden free of squirrels
And the birds up in the air

Jake unwrapping his Christmas presents

Jas is quite ferocious
And when the postman knocks the door
She rips up all the letters
That he drops upon the floor

I pin Granny to the sofa
She can't move without a struggle
So she puts her arms around us
And we have a lovely cuddle

She says that I'm her gorgeous boy
Jas – her cutest little minx
Then we snuggle up together
And we all have forty-winks

She's a soft-touch is our Granny
Lots of doggy-chocs and treats
So when we're sitting round the table
Our tails are wagging at her feet

At meals they like our company
And I like breakfast most
Jas licks Grandad's porridge bowl
And I share Granny's toast

She gives us lovely dinners
Sometimes chicken, sometimes beef
And then we have a chewy-stick
To clean around our teeth

We don't let on to Mum and Dad
The fact that we're spoilt rotten
And our doggy misdemeanours
Are forgiven and forgotten

But our favourite time is Christmas
We get presents, Jas and me
Granny foil-wraps chipolatas
And she hangs them on the tree

There's a present labelled Jakey
(I'm Granny's "bestest" boy)
And another labelled Jasmine
A brand new cuddly toy

We rip off all the wrapping
And the family round us laugh
So we give them licky kisses
And they take our photograph

And from our protected happy homes
We ask the powers above
For all the doggies out there
Like us – cocoon with love

(For our much loved grand-dogs)

JUST DON'T LIGHT MY CANDLE

I know I have a short fuse
My husband tells me so
And as he's the one that's tongue-lashed
I guess he ought to know

I wish I was more tolerant
Even tempered, calm, serene
But there's always one to wind you up
To make you want to scream

There's the supermarket idiot
Parked so close you can't get out
Or takes up disabled places
I could well give them a clout

And when you reach the check-out
They stand there with trolley loads
It says baskets with ten items
My tranquillity explodes

I haven't any patience
And muddles I can't handle
I know my wick is really short
So just don't light my candle

When I wrote this little poem
And my husband took a look
He said "When it comes to lack of patience
You could write a bloody book"

So that's him back in the dog-house
And I'm bristling with high-dudgeon
And if I didn't love him
I'd kill the old curmudgeon

KITCHEN SINK DREAMS

I'm a bored suburban housewife
And want a man with limpid eyes
Who'd not notice all the cellulite
A-quivering on me thighs

So here I stand at kitchen sink
Thoughts burning with desire
For a hunky male – full bloodied
To flame this smouldering fire

With eyes alight with passion
And dribbling with lust
He's rip off all me underwear
And gaze upon me bust

I could lead him up the garden path
And in rubber gloves and bobble hat
We'd mingle in the rhubarb
I'd quite fancy doing that

We could frolic in the new mown hay
And although it would delight us
I'd need some Ibuprofen
'Cos damp brings on my arthritis

I'd be his wanton hussy
He'd be my teddy bear so tender
And I could whip up magic
With strawberry yogurt and a blender

And with my red hot lover
Well, I can only dream
Of what we could get up to
With a can of squirty cream

Aah – I'd have to go out shopping
Before I'd perform the Karma Sutra
The only cream I've got is what
I spread on my verruca

He'd be my rampant tiger
I'd be his naughty turtle dove
I'd tie him to the bed post
And make mad and passionate love

But when we're feeling frisky
In the mood for a good laugh
I'd roll up the daily paper
And whack him with the Telegraph

He'd turn up the heating
And I'd take off me vest
And dance the dance of seven veils
Twirling tassels on me chest

With my illicit lover
We'd canoodle through the night
Before me thermal underwear
Would spark and self-ignite

We'd have high jinks on the table
Cavort upon the kitchen floor
Or swinging from the chandelier
To the strains of Radio Four

He'd buy me flowers and chocolates
And it would give him pleasure
To shower me with diamonds
And little trinkets I could treasure

To a sad neglected housewife
This is as good as it gets
With Romeos few and far between
There's lots of dreaming Juliettes

So I'll get on with the washing-up
But to satisfy my longings
I'll read another chapter of
My book – by Jackie Collins

LED ASTRAY

My wife must really hate me
She's bought me SatNav Doris
Who sits upon the dash-board of
My dear old trusty Morris

Hell's Bells – two women in the car
They're in league to make me suffer
Doris shouts in one ear
And the wife shouts in the other

I fill in map co-ordinates
Told "You've reached your destination"
And I'm wheel deep in wet tarmac
Of some motor-way renovation

I had high hopes of Doris
To help me journey through my life
But she's a sarky bitch dictator
Far worse than any wife

She says "Take the second exit"
That can't be right I shout
Too late – I'm in a car park
It's two pounds fifty to get out

When we approach a junction
She says "Take the next turn right"
Doesn't tell me it's a farm track
Leaves me stuck in mud all night .

She instructs me "Do a U turn now"
I obey – no hesitation
Now I'm parked between two police cars
On the central reservation

She's brought me round in circles
I'd kill if I could see her
This is where she's dumped me
The back entrance of IKEA

This female on her satellite
She then abandons me
To do her nails or wash her hair
Or breaks to drink her tea

She's good at sulky silence
All alone with thoughts I'm stricken
I'm on the road to Cleethorpes
But my destination's Wigan

So let me tell you SatNav Doris
You're getting on my nerves
I'd like a human navigator
Called Lola, blonde with curves

With Lola there beside me
I'd not mind being led astray
She could lead me up a dead end
And have her wicked sexy way

But my wife won't let me
And with Doris I must spend
Hours of recalculating
Until we get there – in the end!

LET THE SQUIRRELS PLAY

See the stark branches of the winter trees
Black against December's sky of coldest blue
Sparkling with the diamond glitter of frost
When the hazy rays of sun peep through

See the red cotoneaster berries blackbirds peck
Timorous snowdrops shivering in virgin white
The gleam of silver ice on the frozen lake
Where sunbeams reflect their pale gold light

See the rainbow prism of a gentle snowflake
Pause - see the beauty of a winters' day
And in the branches of the frosty oak
Let the squirrels play

LOVE THY NEIGHBOUR

We've got a nice size garden
But blocking out the light
Is a mighty great big conifer
Some fifty-feet in height

My husband said he'd chop it
Gave the trunk three hefty whacks
But before he could yell "Timber"
The head flew off the axe

It catapulted through the air
Into next-door's greenhouse crashed
With flying glass and splinters
Every single pane was smashed

Across came Mrs Next-Door
Her face not a pretty sight
With heaving bosoms straining
She was ready for a fight

We said "We're very sorry
For the total decimation"
She was growing lots of green stuff
For her husband's constipation

With face puce and perspiring
Tattooed arms akimbo too
A force that we must reckon with
She's a black belt in kung fu

In an effort to placate her
Well, I thought that it was fitting
So I said that I would hold him
If she would like to hit him

She phoned the local cop-shop
On his bike came Policeman Plod
An when he saw the damage
He called up the riot squad

But in the loud commotion
We forgot the tree half felled
Until the thing came crashing down
Then everybody yelled

It fell on Mrs Next-Door
And although a crane was hired
Before we found her in the branches
She had gurgled and expired

So my husband faced the magistrate
And had to pay for the cremation
Of the flattened Mrs Next-Door
And the conifer excavation

We've given up on gardening
No more trees or flowers or shrubs
We've brightly coloured fishing gnomes
Who fish in little plastic tubs

And we've got brand new neighbours
She's called Mabel, his name's Fred
They've a barricade round their greenhouse
And barbed-wire round their shed

But our new neighbours like to garden
And I can't say that we're pleased
Because all along our boundary fence
They've planted conifer trees.

MAN 'FLU AND HERS

When you feel poorly and nobody cares
No-one cooks dinner or hoovers the stairs
Nobody shops or thinks what to buy
Not a single soul cares if you live or you die
I'm sure that we women aren't meant to be ill
We just hang on in there and take the odd pill
Your head may be splitting and all your joints aching
You grit your teeth bravely though your spirit's breaking
Smile through each dizzy spell 'til it passes
Dismiss your headache – Say "I just need new glasses"
With shivers and flushes – you suffer the 'flu
And plough on regardless – that's what women do.

The first sign of a sniffle men take to their bed
With moaning and groaning that they'll soon be dead
Get my prescription and ring up the Doc
My feet are freezing, where's my woolly socks
Heat up some whisky to put in my tea
Must I walk to the bathroom when I want to wee
Fetch me some linctus and cod-liver oil
Best take my temperature, I'm starting to boil
No-one has ever been this ill before
So creep round me quietly and don't slam the door
My chest is all wheezy – is that death rattle too
I think I'll expire with this nasty man-flu

My nose is all red and runny and raw
I'd shove some Vick up it but it's much too sore
Get me more aspirin and where's the Night Nurse
And smooth my brow gently, I'm feeling much worse
My tongue is all furry and just feel my glands
Now I've got pins and needles in both of my hands
Bring me more whisky in warming hot milk
And play soothing music – No – Not Acker Bilk
Bring clean pyjamas, I'm staying in bed
Prop up my pillow for my aching head
And while you're at it, please plug into Sky
I want to watch "footie" as I slowly die

I'm much too poorly to get up and dress
Now I've spilled oil of camphor all over my vest
No – I can't wash it off, I'll just lay here and smell
And please come much faster when I ring my bell
I'm getting a rash, and look – are they spots
My eyes have gone fuzzy – with flashing red dots
Please don't call your mother - the rotten old trout
Do you think the pain in my knee could be gout
Yes, I hear what you're saying, you've had it too
But with my influenza – I'm much worse than you
The virus has two strains and when it occurs
There's one labelled "man-flu" and one labelled "hers"

MICK THE MARTIAN

My name is Mick the Martian
I come from outer space
To visit this weird clan on earth
That's called the human race

I don't think much of your system
On procreation I have data
That tells me men have all the fun
And the wife pays nine months later

Here on Mars we're unisex
But I'll tell you – just between us
We lean towards the masculine
Since the girls all left for Venus

When we want to multiply
Our production line will mass produce
A myriad of little Martians
In blue and lime and puce

I'm both masculine and feminine
And to preserve my mental health
I've got an on-off button
So I can't argue with myself

Your process for activation
Would drive me round the bend
You shovel food into your gob
Then push it out the other end

You breed four legged creatures
Called pig and cow and sheep
Then you take them to the abattoir
Turn them into meat to eat

I just can't see the sense in that
Me – I'm plugged into the mains
To computerise my system
And programme all my brains

If I'm needing extra energy
Or feeling somewhat sporty
My Mum will get the oil can out
And squirt me with W-D 40

To navigate and circulate
Your method is bizarre
You're strapped inside a metal box
Some contraption called a car

Me – I've got a jet-pack
And I whizz from place to place
Be it Timbuctoo or Clacton
Or planet hop in outer space

I've got one eye and stubby legs
And a button on my belly
And if I give it a quick twiddle
I can watch your world on telly

I've got a round green body
From which hangs a dangly widget
Which comes in rather handy
As I can open beer cans with it

I've only got one central eye
And a nice bright red proboscis
My toes are all of different lengths
It's called myxoma**toes**is

Your world is not a friendly place
You're not yet civilised
You still have those upon your earth
Who kill and terrorise

And so I'll leave you earthlings
And through a galaxy of stars
I'll fly my flying saucer
'Till I get back home to Mars

<u>MISCONCEPTION</u>

We have eleven children
And I don't want any more
If we go on at this rate
We'll end up with a score

Perhaps it's time to have 'the snip'
Because I think that it is meant
To stop unwanted pregnancies
And more babies will prevent

So I had this vasectomy
But didn't read the small print, maybe?
Because it simply gave the wife
A different coloured baby

MOONBEAM IN MY HEART

The fulfilment of my existence
A child, conceived in love and joy
Wonderment – completes my being
My baby, my son, my boy

But now in darkness I'm engulfed
No cocoon of safety did my womb provide
No butterfly movement ever felt
Taken – not held safely there to thrive

I feel a guilt I can't assuage
An aching emptiness I can't convey
The coldness of bereavement
From my imperfect body – torn away

I think; I try to come to terms
But my eyes with tears still flood
A life, a foetus, a beating heart
Washed away in tidal blood

Why was his birth not in God's plan
My unborn child and I to part
Never to hold him in my arms
Forever a moonbeam in my heart

MOONLIGHT LINK TO WHITBY BAY

The Sea Nymph sails high
On glittering water
The catch is small
Mean times
Tempest that shows no mercy

Seventeen-fifty-three
Whales evade us
In Artic ice
They blow and go
And survive the harpoon throw

Come dawn the town will welcome
The whaling ship
No bounty
A hard winter
But thank God their men are home

Eyes traverse the silver ribbon
On moonlit waves
To the shore
Where she waits
'Neath the Abbey, in Whitby Bay

Photo by
Jamie Parry

<u>NOTHING ON THE TELLY</u>

There's a hundred telly programmes
But not one you'd want to see
Just rude and puerile rubbish
That masquerades as comedy

Do you remember Love Thy Neighbour?
Or 'Till Death Us Do Part?
And each week we watched Steptoe
Rag and bone, and horse and cart

How we laughed at Porridge
And Hi-de-Hi we did enjoy
Dad's Army, Captain Mainwaring
With Private Pike, the stupid boy

And Some Mothers Do 'Ave 'Em
Stunts that took our breath away
And the classic Fools and Horses
Still watched on Gold today

How we laugh at plonker Rodney
And Del Boy, the dodgy dealer
From Paris, New York, Peckham
Clapped-out yellow old three wheeler

We made models with Blue Peter
And if you remember back
We gathered round a ten-inch screen
To see our favourite – Crackerjack

Do you remember The Two Ronnies?
Reggie Perrin, Rising Damp
And It Ain't Half Hot Mum
In the Indian army camp

But nowadays it's Casualty
No Holby City then
'Cos for our dose of drama
We watched Emergency Ward Ten

We heard Basil rant in Fawlty Towers
With Manuel from Barcelona
Hancock - back in sixty-one
In the scene from The Blood Donor

Now we've dreary cooking demos
So called 'comedy' – assorted
And I really wish that Mrs Brown
Had had her boys aborted

You never heard the 'F' word
Cringed at 'reality' TV
They've banned some shows we used to love
They're not correct – politically

I know it's age related
And, yes, I do remember Muffin
But you can put your modern tripe
Where the turkey puts his stuffing

Bring back Mary Whitehouse
She'd censor all obscenity
Our only consolation is
We get our licence FREE

Now the screen sits in the corner
Fifty inches, with HD
But there's nothing on the telly
For the likes of you and me

PANSY, MANDY AND KATE

Kate, an Australian kangaroo
Was tired of living in London Zoo
So she caught a bus up the Marylebone Road
Down to a pub called "The Frog and The Toad"
With Pansy, a piglet, ex-silver-screen star
A brave refugee from the town's abattoir
And Mandy, the meerkat, of late T.V. fame
The trio were playing their dominoes game

But as kangaroo, piglet and meerkat called Mandy
With three coloured straws knocked back lager shandy
Said they'd had enough of their sworn indenture
All craved excitement and real world adventure
The three musketeers then got back on the bus
They all had their passes, so that was a plus
And down to the river to look for a boat
Anything they could steer and would float

They soon found a rowing boat painted bright blue
To row round the world – that's what they would do
So Pansy and Mandy each grabbed an oar
And Kangaroo Kate pushed them off from the shore
Into the swell of the great River Thames
Through cities and country, where ever it wends
They stopped for provisions - not wanting to grouch,
Katie stored chocolate and cake in her pouch

Soon the three friends left the Thames estuary
To boldly head out on a cold choppy sea
They planned and took turns, each to navigate
So all manned the oars and helped calculate
To where their adventure would finally lead
Ahoy, hoist the sail, farewell, and God Speed
So Pansy, the piglet, and meerkat called Mandy
Set off with Kate, and some apricot brandy

With sails and buckets and oars in the locks
Soon left the drabness of old English docks
Like Columbus and Drake and Ferdy Magellan
Planned to sail to the tropics - live on water-melon
The sea was deep blue and bright sun-shine shone
Soon they reached the mouth of the great Amazon
There pink Pansy Piglet met Crocodile Fred
And with jollification they were quickly wed

But as dawn was breaking on their wedded bliss
She left poor old Fred with not even a kiss
From mascaraed eyes – carefully not to smear
She wiped away a sly crocodile tear
Said "I'm off to meet Alfonse, a cute Alligator
In the reptile world, he's the new hot potato"
Mandy and Kate – said they thought it unwise
But Pansy turned a deaf ear to their cries

Then off she headed to meet her new beau
Across the Amazon's mighty flow
With water-wings punctured - she started to sink
Katie and Mandy pulled her back from the brink
And Pansy, the piglet, so full of remorse
Cooked them all dinner, then she set the course
To the Caribbean where rogue pirates waited
And in three little bodies a great fear pulsated

But Katie, the bravest out of the three
Said "You leave that Captain Hook unto me"
With 'come-hither eyes' and wiggling shank
She lured the bold pirate right up his own plank
With his lusty intent and a leer quite depraved
Katie shoved him into a watery grave
Then she tossed all the pirates to barracuda
And their ship to the Triangle in Bermuda

Said Meerkat Mandy, "That's enough adventure
Much more of this I'll be getting dementia
I've forgotten a world where nothing will happen
Let's share a council flat somewhere in Clapham
We can eat fish and chips every day and grow fat"
Said Katie and Pansy "Sounds good, does that"
"And every night we'll sleep sound in our bed
And watch our adventure on telly instead"

So the tireless trio then headed home
Heads full of adventure but no more to roam
So if you're a visitor, come to the city
And you've enough money to put in the kitty
Take a jaunt to 'The Frog and The Toad'
Your find it at the end of the Marylebone Road
You'll meet Pansy, Mandy and Kate in the throes
Counting the spots on the same dominoes

PEARLY GATES

The entrance to our heaven
Is guarded by a Pearly Gate
And if you want to enter
You must ring the bell and wait

Along will come St. Peter
And you must justify
If you're fit to enter heaven
Or sent down below to fry

So when a group of Travellers
Came into St. Peter's view
It put him in a quandary
And he pondered what to do

Invite them in or send them down
While he took time to hesitate
The Travellers did a runner
And they nicked the Pearly Gate

PERKS IN THE PAIL

I am a window cleaner
You'd never guess the sights I've seen
With my chamois at the ready
And my can of Windowlene

'Cos while I'm up my ladder
Through the glass I look and see
All the many faults and foibles
Of Tweedledum and Tweedledee

First viewed through dirty windows
A pillar of society
Is a renowned politician
And his under-secretary

Tip-toeing through his tulips
This queen of great pretenders
Is prancing round his hot-house
In fishnets and suspenders

Next - a peep through rectory nets
Well, I was thunder-struck
In the bath there sat the vicar
Playing with his rubber duck

And peering in at Number Ten
There's banker – Horace Bassett
Head to head with Widow Swanky
Warming up her frozen assets

Across the road the spinster sisters
Who've lived a life devoid of sin
Are watching saucy movies
While knocking back the gin

And I've caught Councillor Hardy
A big-wig, full of pomp
With the check-out girl from Tesco's
In a naughty bed-room romp

I've spied the local doctor
Who's supposed to cure all ills
Swallowing free samples
Of his own Viagra pills

Best of all, I saw the Mayor
Chain of Office dangling down
Cavorting round the boudoir
With a "Lady of the Town"

And when I've cleaned their windows
A knowing wink tells what I've seen
That although their glass is sparkling
Their lives aren't squeaky-clean

Now I've retired from window cleaning
I'm into blackmail – it's quite funny
Because instead of murky water
My pail's brimming with hush-money

PIETY CAN WAIT

Said the Actress to the Bishop
"Please pray for my salvation
A word from you will save me
From hell-fire and damnation"

Said the Bishop to the Actress
"I've committed greater sin
But the Good Lord will forgive us
And I'm sure he'll let us in

So let's wait 'till we're in heaven
Then our sins we will repent
Come, my dear, make whoopee
'Till our time on earth is spent"

POLITICAL CORRECTNESS

I don't do Political Correctness
And if you listen when I speak
I've an affliction – it's called Foot and Mouth
Because into mouth I put my feet

It's all down to confusion
Black or white's OK to say
But you can't say brown or yellow
Or call a happy fellow gay

There's ageism and sexism
Racism - that's not all
I'm sure there's other isms
That I simply can't recall

As a child I had a golly-wog
And I loved him to bits
And I had a doll called Noddy
Banned by political nitwits

Men and woman of this nation
Died giving us Freedom of Speech
So ignore political correctness
And the idiocy they preach

You're entitled to opinion
Get on your soap box – light the fuse
It's the thought behind the saying
Not the choice of words you use

No-one should seek to hurt others
Or insult a creed or race
But Political Correctness
Has gone mad – it's a disgrace

RESOLUTIONS OF A SPINSTER

I'm a spinster of this parish
And no longer in my prime
My resolution is to find a man
Before the bells of New Year chime

I've put an advert in the paper
To find my perfect mate
And with my brand new lover
The New Year we'll celebrate

I've dreams of our first meeting
Perhaps an Italian Ristorante
A small secluded table
Drinking glasses of chianti

And now I've waited patiently
Received my first reply
And although I've read it carefully
He's just not my sort of guy

His photo's no oil painting
And I've got serious doubts
He want us to meet in Asda
Alongside the Brussels sprouts

A secret assignation
So romantic would be fine
But he thinks Kentucky Chicken
I think candle-light and wine

I'm contemplating what to wear
A slinky number – sexy – black
He's planning socks and sandals
And a grubby anorak

I want to dance in moonlight
I can't see him doing that
Because his arms are too short
And his body much too fat

I'm dreaming Porsche, Ferrari
Cars favoured by rich blokes
He's only got an ancient bike
And that's got rusty spokes

He could fly me to the Seychelles
On white sand speak words erotic
But a caravan in Bognor
That's his idea of exotic

We could buy a posh apartment
A London love-nest – so bijou
But he's a bed-sit down in Acton
With Wormwood Scrubs in view

I think champagne and caviar
Soft kisses lingering on my lips
But he's thinking of a one night stand
Then be off for pie and chips

I want a man of substance
With a shed-load in the bank
Who can't wait to share it with me
Not this hard-up gormless plank

Do I really need this muppet
I've thought it over with some care
But two hours in his company
And I'd be pulling out my hair

My resolution's doomed to failure
And in my heart I fear
In a lonely, cold and empty bed
I'll face another blooming year!

REVENGE

It's the ultimate betrayal
He's run off with "office bird"
They're flying to Barbados
Is the last thing that I heard

Good riddance now he's left me
And I don't care if he snogged her
But to take her to Barbados
When he just took me to Bognor!

Now louse and tart have checked-in
But when they reach security
They'll be a surprise waiting
A parting gift from me

They'll hear the snap of latex gloves
That'll make his eyes water
With a strip-search for the hussy
Young enough to be his daughter

Because I 'phoned up the air-port
Told customs – when they checked 'em
That he's got cocaine hidden
In a packet – up his rectum!

SAT-NAV SUSIE

My husband, like all other men
When lost won't ask directions
So I've bought him a SatNav
With satellite connections

She's quite authoritarian
No nonsense to allow
When he chooses to ignore her
She says "Do a U-Turn - Now"

When we approach a roundabout
And she says "Take the Second Exit"
He shouts and argues with her
Complains that she's dyslexic

And so she gets her own back
And drives him round the bend
Stuck up a one-way alley
Single lane – with a dead end!

And me – I sit here quietly
Watch the traffic, do my knitting
He can yell at SatNav Susie
Map read? – not me – I'm quitting!

SILENT SANDALS

Once again the nightmare grips me
I'm bathed in sweat with fright
See creeping, silent sandals
Prowling through the night

I'm a little boy of seven
Sleeping in a dormitory
There's half a dozen others
But I know he'll pick on me

I still see his silhouette
In the darkened corridor
Silent sandals move towards me
Across the dusty wooden floor

He says I am his special friend
I must promise not to tell
And if I break the secret
I'll burn in everlasting hell

I know that he will take me
And it's no use to beg
Fear knots inside my body
Warm urine trickles down my leg

I feel his breath upon me
But our eyes never meet
I hang me head in shame; tears drip
On the sandals on his feet

Today I am a grown man
And I face him in the court
But the victory is hollow
As to justice he is brought

Guilty is the verdict
But this is no recompense
However long the sentence
I lost childhood innocence

Now he is an old man
Ravaged by depravity
But those creeping, silent sandals
Have the power to still haunt me

<u>SOLACE</u>

You're no longer here beside me
My heart breaks with silent screams
From the nightmare of my day-time
I'll find solace in my dreams

<u>SOOTY SANTA</u>

Santa got stuck up the chimney
You couldn't see him for soot
Shaking it here; blowing it there
Huffing and puffing everywhere
Reindeers stuck in the fire-breast
The presents fell into the grate
But we must rescue Santa
Before we celebrate

SPELL-CHECKER

I'm Major Aubrey Flunkett
And I'm writing to protest
Of the police investigation
And my subsequent arrest

I wrote a letter to the vicar
To thank him for his donation
To the home for wayward women
And his thoughts for their salvation

I used to have a secretary
To whom I could dictate
But now I've a computer
And the feeling's mutual hate

This miscarriage of justice
Is very plain to see
Was the fault of my spell-checker
And yet you all blame me

They said my letter broke the law
Its meaning was obscene
Because I didn't stop to check
The spelling on the screen

I had to give a statement
Its accuracy sworn
Then they took away my hard-drive
To examine it for porn

I told them I'm important
And said it would be quicker
To drop the charge against me
And interrogate the vicar

Perhaps I'll face a caution
Or a prison term suspended
It's because of my computer
That I'm wrongly apprehended

They searched the house for girly mags
And pictures – saucy, skittish
I've told them it's outrageous
There's no sex here – I'm British

My simple "thank-you" letter
And the mix-up in translation
Was not intended to promote
A breach of legislation

In good faith I called the vicar
An "eloquent public speaker"
But my spell-checker changed it to
An *"elegant pubic squeaker"*

THE ADULTERER

I can smell the sex upon you
The perfume of her embrace
As you creep into bed beside me
And tears trickle down my face

I spare you explanations
As I secretly feign sleep
But inside my heart is breaking
As so silently I weep

Will the time come that you tell me
That our marriage vows you'll break
I lay there fraught with tension
And with apprehension wait

When was it you stopped loving me
What reason – tell me why
When did we drift so far apart
When did joy and laughter die

Each to our own side of the bed
No more our limbs enfold
A chilly distance separates
The fire, once bright, now cold

Who is she, this marriage wrecker
Is a life apart to be my fate
I lie in dread and trepidation
Of this female that I hate

When will guilt make you tell me
That it's her you now hold dear
Then pack your bags and walk away
I face a future full of fear

My heart cries out in anguish
And I curse the stars above
For this void of space between us
And this cruelty called love

THE GIRL AT THE BUS-STOP

This beauty at the bus-stop
Is a vision of delight
My sun-beam on a cloudy day
My dream of every night

I see her from the window of
My third-floor office cell
She's the power to mesmerise me
All day on her thoughts dwell

I'm gazing down upon her
From my vantage point above
Each day newly captivated
By an all-consuming love

I'll never get to know her name
Perhaps it's Rose, or maybe Lily
Or where the bus will take her
Leicester Square or Piccadilly

She wearing summer sandals
And a pretty dress – so neat
And I think of my wife Gladys
With her clomping Size Eight feet

I don't know why I married Gladys
She's as miserable as sin
Mean and fat and ugly
With hair growing out her chin

Adoring eyes fix on my Venus
Each morning standing there
Waiting for the bus to stop
The girl with golden hair

In fantasy I hold her hand
She's warm in my embrace
I feel the soft touch of her cheek
And gently kiss her face

I see the bus approaching
The damn thing's there on time
Now I'll wait four hours and twenty
Before once more she's mine

I turn back to my computer
The daily grind I must begin
Then plod back home to Gladys
And her bloody hairy chin

THE HIROSHIMA QUESTION

Across the valley the bomber came
On that summer Monday morn
August 6th, nineteen-forty-five
Hiroshima's death-filled dawn

It had flown from Tinian Island
The U.S. Marianas base
And dropped a bomb called "Little Boy"
On an unsuspecting race

The B-twenty-nine released its load
At six-fifteen that fateful day
Annihilation of the innocent
Then turned and flew away

Now so many years have passed
And the outcome scrutinised
It's true the war was shortened
But one-hundred-thousand died

Was it right to bomb the people
To see their charred remains
To mass-kill a population
Radiation death still claims

In war there is dilemma
Still descendants moralise
That children tore off burning flesh
To save many allied lives

There cannot be an answer
Was it right or was it wrong
The day the plane – Enola Gay
Dropped the first atomic bomb

THE JOURNEY

The white light beckons
Through translucent mist
Coercing me
Do not resist
Fear not this journey

Magnetism strong
But I'm not ready
Waver, dither
Hold me steady
I fear this journey

Focus my brain
And hold fast my will
Surge strong my blood
My heart not still
I fight this journey

The light diffuses
No longer tunnelled
Lungs heave, breathe
No more pummelled
Too soon – this journey

My eyes shoot open
Blessed relief – above
Harsh strip lighting
I see my love
Journey's end – **here** – not there

THE OLD GOOSE

My husband had a lover
And at first I was quite sad
But what's good for goose and gander
Meant it's not turned out too bad

She was blonde and nubile
Without care and fancy free
But she didn't get her porridge
'Cos I put bromide in his tea

With the wrath of woman scorned
His plans I meant to scupper
So I laced his oats with garlic
And he ate them for his supper

I turned on all the water works
With screams and sulks and rants
But then I just got even
Put itching powder in his pants

I put chip fat in his hair-spray
In cabbage water boiled his vest
And fish oil in deodorant
Which he sprayed upon his chest

I fed him lots of laxatives
And to enhance their thrills
When they spent the night together
I added sleeping pills

She soon dumped this sugar-daddy
'Though he never cottoned-on
Why the fire that flamed his ego
Fizzled out and all went wrong

Now I've emptied out the bank account
Left a note for Casanova
And I'm off to Honolulu
With my toy-boy – it's all over

THE 'STUPID' PRIZE

If there's an annual prize for 'stupid'
This year's will surely go
To a power-crazed Parking Warden
Short of body, wits of slow

We bought an 'all-day' ticket
And displayed it on our screen
But **this** height-challenged warden
Said the time could not be seen

The screen on our old motor-home
Stands higher than a car
But we could read the details
From quite a distance far

She said that it was our fault
We had laid the ticket flat
And you can't argue with a 'jobs-worth'
In a Parking Wardens' hat

"Do you think Welsh parking tickets
Can stand of their own volition
To pirouette across the dash board
And present in pole position?"

Unimpressed by my sarcasm
And even though I tried to show her
She wasn't tall enough and said
"You should display your ticket lower"

And so the fine was issued
Beside the River Dee
By a uniformed Welsh dragon
With the I.Q. of a pea

Congratulations Parking Warden
You get the 'Stupid' prize
We'll refuse to pay your parking fine
'Til the stars fall from the skies

And to your Welsh employers
Please hire wardens who are taller
Or provide a small step-ladder
For the dumpy and the smaller

TOLD YOU SO

When God in Heaven designed Adam
He hadn't thought of Eve
But then he pinched a rib or two
And a female was conceived

Now herein lies the problem
Adam only had a single brain
So God took just one half of it
To divide it was his aim

The left side he gave to Adam
That move was really bright
Because women had the other side
And that's why we're always right!

TRIBUTE TO ADA LOVELACE
1815 - 1852

When Lord Byron saw his daughter
The mewling new born cry to hear
It never crossed his mind she'd be
A renowned pioneer

Born to George and Isabella
Eighteen-fifteen, tenth December
This girl child was a genius
The whole world would remember

With her image on our passports
As we travel far and wide
She's a scientific legend
Forever at our side

With great mathematical ability
Analyst, metaphysician
For a mechanical computer
She designed an algorithm

Her workings with Charles Babbage
On his Engine Analytical
She had a vision of computers
And imagination critical

In schools up and down the country
In each assembly hall
To encourage girls in science
You'll find her picture on the wall

In educational establishments
The IT department will proclaim
She's the first computer programmer
And Ada Lovelace is her name

So when we switch on our computers
And view technology today
Forgive a touch of female pride
But our Ada paved the way

UNDERWEAR OF YESTER-YEAR

Remember camphorated oil?
The smell still lingers on my chest
And my grandmother knitting me
An itchy woollen vest

With a petticoat of flannel
And knickers winceyette
A top coat made of gabardine
Hat, gloves, scarf – a matching set

And what about the liberty bodice?
Rubber fasteners in a row
With small suspender buttons
Hanging down there – just below

Once I been camphorated
And firmly stitched in mine
The thing remained in situ
Through winter 'til spring-time

Remember whale-bone corsets
Thank God, I just missed those
And when I was liberated
I jumped into panti-hose

But enough's enough, it's gone too far
Last week I got it wrong
I thought I'd be quite trendy
So I bought myself a thong

Well, we all learn by our mistakes
Let me tell you – I can vouch
They cut you up like cheese-wire
If you try to sit or crouch

So while you're listening to me
I'll ask where I can get
Some warm and fleecy underwear
In old-fashioned winceyette?

UNISEX BRAIN

There's much talk about mixed gender
It's a subject quite complex
But male or female – what a muddle
If your brain is unisex

One side says "Eat Chocolate"
"You deserve a little treat"
The other side says it's OK
To splash the toilet seat

The female side spends money
On lipstick, handbags, shoes
The male side rarely thinks beyond
Football, sex and booze

The left side, that's the male part
Wears pants and socks in bed
Leaves dirty washing on the floor
Holds his plate out to be fed

On the right, and full of mystery
Will calm and dormant lie
A brain calculating coldly
How to strangle him with his tie

So in a brain that's unisex
Will the left and right sides fight
Will the circuits fuse together
Self-combust and then ignite

VICARS AND TARTS

We've a party invitation
To meet the neighbours, Tim and Tess
It's seven-thirty Saturday
Quite informal – fancy dress

We could go as 'tarts and vicars'
My wife had this bright idea
She would wear her shortest mini
And I could hire vicar's gear

Getting warmed up to the theme
I thought it quite a lark
If the wife went as the vicar
And I went as the tart

So with gaiters and dog collar
My wife dressed for the night
But with hairy legs through fishnets
I was not a pretty sight

A wonder-bra enhanced my chest
In mini-skirt I looked the part
With strappy top and killer heels
I was the tartiest of tarts

So we arrived together
At our neighbour's – Tess and Tim
I thought they looked a bit surprised
But politely asked us in

There at the dinner table
Another vicar and his hussy
A shame we'd had the same idea
But, never mind, I wasn't fussy

I said "Hey Vic, you're looking good
But your tart needs much more bling
If she's that po-faced all evening
She'll never make the party swing"

Then Tim made introductions
"Councillor Prim and Reverend Peek
You've come on the wrong evening
Fancy dress is Saturday week"

<u>WISHFUL THINKING</u>

I'd like to be a secret agent
A modern Mata Hari
The government would reward me with
A shiny red Ferrari

Or I could be a politician
And "Let me make this clear"
When it came to the election
I'd say things you'd want to hear

What about a high court judge
On bench, with wig and gown
I'd sentence thugs to twenty years
Hard labour – "Take him down"

But I'm just a lowly writer
Of poetry to be precise
While it's nice to be important
It's more important to be nice

#0172 - 170616 - C0 - 210/148/6 - PB - DID1488601